The contents of this journal are

PERSONAL

and

CONFIDENTIAL.

DO NOT READ.

If found, please return to:

Phone number:

The Runner's Workout Log

by

Alex Haddox, M.Ed.

Published by

Palladium Education,® Inc.
6520 Platt Avenue, #174
West Hills, CA 91307-3218
PalladiumEducation.com

Copyright © 2016 by Palladium Education,® Inc.

Except as permitted under the Copyright Act of 1976, no part of this book may be reproduced by any electronic or mechanical means in any form including the use of information storage and retrieval systems, without permission in writing from the copyright owner.

Trademarks: "Palladium Education", and the Palladium Education, Inc. logo are trademarks of Palladium Education,® Inc.

ISBN-13:   978-1-939408-39-6

ISBN-10:   1-939408-39-3

To all my coaches who tried to make me a better runner.

...and failed through no fault of their own.

Sometimes you just suck at a sport.

The Runner's Workout Log

Table of Contents

How to Use This Log..iii

Sample Log Entry iv

Training Log... 1-95

Body Composition Log (skinfold)..................................97

Body Measurements Log 97

Weight Log 99-100

How to Use This Log

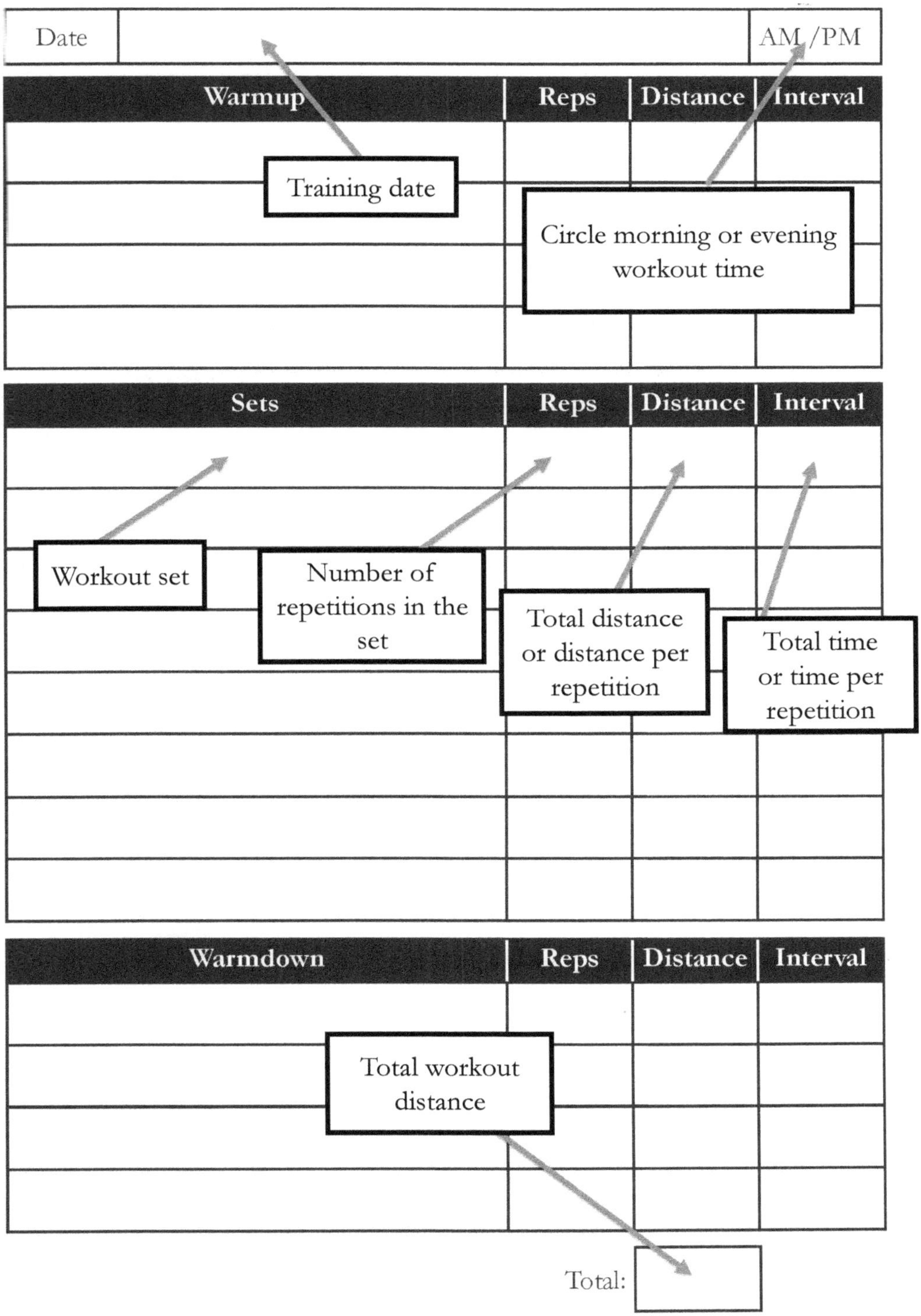

The Runner's Workout Log

Date				AM/PM

Warmup	Reps	Distance	Interval

Training date

Circle morning or evening workout time

Sets	Reps	Distance	Interval

Workout set

Number of repetitions in the set

Total distance or distance per repetition

Total time or time per repetition

Warmdown	Reps	Distance	Interval

Total workout distance

Total:

PalladiumEducation.com

iii

The Runner's Workout Log

Sample Log Entry

Date	7/14/2016			AM/**PM**

Warmup	Reps	Distance	Interval
JOG	1	800	:20
RUN	8	100	:20

Sets	Reps	Distance	Interval
FARTLEK	8	200	
STAIRS	6		
TABATA	10	(20)	:10
PYRAMID	3	200 800	:10

Warmdown	Reps	Distance	Interval
JOG	1	800	:30
JOG	1	600	:30
JOG	1	200	:30

Total: 13,700

The Runner's Workout Log

Date		AM /PM

Warmup	Reps	Distance	Interval

Sets	Reps	Distance	Interval

Warmdown	Reps	Distance	Interval

Total:

PalladiumEducation.com

The Runner's Workout Log

Date		AM /PM

Warmup	Reps	Distance	Interval

Sets	Reps	Distance	Interval

Warmdown	Reps	Distance	Interval

Total:

Palladium Education,® Inc.

The Runner's Workout Log

Date		AM /PM

Warmup	Reps	Distance	Interval

Sets	Reps	Distance	Interval

Warmdown	Reps	Distance	Interval

Total:

PalladiumEducation.com

The Runner's Workout Log

Date		AM /PM

Warmup	Reps	Distance	Interval

Sets	Reps	Distance	Interval

Warmdown	Reps	Distance	Interval

Total:

Palladium Education,® Inc.

The Runner's Workout Log

Date		AM /PM

Warmup	Reps	Distance	Interval

Sets	Reps	Distance	Interval

Warmdown	Reps	Distance	Interval

Total:

The Runner's Workout Log

Date		AM /PM

Warmup	Reps	Distance	Interval

Sets	Reps	Distance	Interval

Warmdown	Reps	Distance	Interval

Total:

Palladium Education,® Inc.

The Runner's Workout Log

Date		AM /PM

Warmup	Reps	Distance	Interval

Sets	Reps	Distance	Interval

Warmdown	Reps	Distance	Interval

Total:

The Runner's Workout Log

Date		AM /PM

Warmup	Reps	Distance	Interval

Sets	Reps	Distance	Interval

Warmdown	Reps	Distance	Interval

Total:

Palladium Education,® Inc.

The Runner's Workout Log

Date		AM /PM

Warmup	Reps	Distance	Interval

Sets	Reps	Distance	Interval

Warmdown	Reps	Distance	Interval

Total:

The Runner's Workout Log

Date		AM /PM

Warmup	Reps	Distance	Interval

Sets	Reps	Distance	Interval

Warmdown	Reps	Distance	Interval

Total:

The Runner's Workout Log

Date		AM /PM

Warmup	Reps	Distance	Interval

Sets	Reps	Distance	Interval

Warmdown	Reps	Distance	Interval

Total:

The Runner's Workout Log

Date		AM /PM

Warmup	Reps	Distance	Interval

Sets	Reps	Distance	Interval

Warmdown	Reps	Distance	Interval

Total:

The Runner's Workout Log

Date		AM /PM

Warmup	Reps	Distance	Interval

Sets	Reps	Distance	Interval

Warmdown	Reps	Distance	Interval

Total:

The Runner's Workout Log

Date		AM /PM

Warmup	Reps	Distance	Interval

Sets	Reps	Distance	Interval

Warmdown	Reps	Distance	Interval

Total:

The Runner's Workout Log

Date		AM /PM

Warmup	Reps	Distance	Interval

Sets	Reps	Distance	Interval

Warmdown	Reps	Distance	Interval

Total:

The Runner's Workout Log

Date		AM /PM

Warmup	Reps	Distance	Interval

Sets	Reps	Distance	Interval

Warmdown	Reps	Distance	Interval

Total:

Palladium Education,® Inc.

The Runner's Workout Log

Date		AM /PM

Warmup	Reps	Distance	Interval

Sets	Reps	Distance	Interval

Warmdown	Reps	Distance	Interval

Total:

The Runner's Workout Log

Date		AM /PM

Warmup	Reps	Distance	Interval

Sets	Reps	Distance	Interval

Warmdown	Reps	Distance	Interval

Total:

Palladium Education,® Inc.

The Runner's Workout Log

Date		AM /PM

Warmup	Reps	Distance	Interval

Sets	Reps	Distance	Interval

Warmdown	Reps	Distance	Interval

Total:

The Runner's Workout Log

Date		AM /PM

Warmup	Reps	Distance	Interval

Sets	Reps	Distance	Interval

Warmdown	Reps	Distance	Interval

Total:

The Runner's Workout Log

Date		AM /PM

Warmup	Reps	Distance	Interval

Sets	Reps	Distance	Interval

Warmdown	Reps	Distance	Interval

Total:

The Runner's Workout Log

Date		AM /PM

Warmup	Reps	Distance	Interval

Sets	Reps	Distance	Interval

Warmdown	Reps	Distance	Interval

Total:

The Runner's Workout Log

Date		AM /PM

Warmup	Reps	Distance	Interval

Sets	Reps	Distance	Interval

Warmdown	Reps	Distance	Interval

Total:

The Runner's Workout Log

Date		AM /PM

Warmup	Reps	Distance	Interval

Sets	Reps	Distance	Interval

Warmdown	Reps	Distance	Interval

Total:

Palladium Education,® Inc.

The Runner's Workout Log

Date				AM /PM

Warmup	**Reps**	**Distance**	**Interval**

Sets	**Reps**	**Distance**	**Interval**

Warmdown	**Reps**	**Distance**	**Interval**

Total:

The Runner's Workout Log

Date		AM /PM

Warmup	Reps	Distance	Interval

Sets	Reps	Distance	Interval

Warmdown	Reps	Distance	Interval

Total:

The Runner's Workout Log

Date		AM /PM

Warmup	Reps	Distance	Interval

Sets	Reps	Distance	Interval

Warmdown	Reps	Distance	Interval

Total:

The Runner's Workout Log

Date		AM /PM

Warmup	Reps	Distance	Interval

Sets	Reps	Distance	Interval

Warmdown	Reps	Distance	Interval

Total:

The Runner's Workout Log

Date		AM /PM

Warmup	Reps	Distance	Interval

Sets	Reps	Distance	Interval

Warmdown	Reps	Distance	Interval

Total:

The Runner's Workout Log

Date		AM /PM

Warmup	Reps	Distance	Interval

Sets	Reps	Distance	Interval

Warmdown	Reps	Distance	Interval

Total:

The Runner's Workout Log

Date		AM /PM

Warmup	Reps	Distance	Interval

Sets	Reps	Distance	Interval

Warmdown	Reps	Distance	Interval

Total:

PalladiumEducation.com

The Runner's Workout Log

Date		AM /PM

Warmup	Reps	Distance	Interval

Sets	Reps	Distance	Interval

Warmdown	Reps	Distance	Interval

Total:

Palladium Education,® Inc.

The Runner's Workout Log

Date		AM /PM

Warmup	Reps	Distance	Interval

Sets	Reps	Distance	Interval

Warmdown	Reps	Distance	Interval

Total:

The Runner's Workout Log

Date		AM /PM

Warmup	Reps	Distance	Interval

Sets	Reps	Distance	Interval

Warmdown	Reps	Distance	Interval

Total:

The Runner's Workout Log

Date		AM /PM

Warmup	Reps	Distance	Interval

Sets	Reps	Distance	Interval

Warmdown	Reps	Distance	Interval

Total:

The Runner's Workout Log

Date		AM /PM

Warmup	Reps	Distance	Interval

Sets	Reps	Distance	Interval

Warmdown	Reps	Distance	Interval

Total:

The Runner's Workout Log

Date		AM /PM

Warmup	Reps	Distance	Interval

Sets	Reps	Distance	Interval

Warmdown	Reps	Distance	Interval

Total:

The Runner's Workout Log

Date		AM /PM

Warmup	Reps	Distance	Interval

Sets	Reps	Distance	Interval

Warmdown	Reps	Distance	Interval

Total:

The Runner's Workout Log

Date		AM /PM

Warmup	Reps	Distance	Interval

Sets	Reps	Distance	Interval

Warmdown	Reps	Distance	Interval

Total:

The Runner's Workout Log

Date		AM /PM

Warmup	Reps	Distance	Interval

Sets	Reps	Distance	Interval

Warmdown	Reps	Distance	Interval

Total:

The Runner's Workout Log

Date		AM /PM

Warmup	Reps	Distance	Interval

Sets	Reps	Distance	Interval

Warmdown	Reps	Distance	Interval

Total:

The Runner's Workout Log

Date		AM /PM

Warmup	Reps	Distance	Interval

Sets	Reps	Distance	Interval

Warmdown	Reps	Distance	Interval

Total:

The Runner's Workout Log

Date		AM /PM

Warmup	Reps	Distance	Interval

Sets	Reps	Distance	Interval

Warmdown	Reps	Distance	Interval

Total:

The Runner's Workout Log

Date		AM /PM

Warmup	Reps	Distance	Interval

Sets	Reps	Distance	Interval

Warmdown	Reps	Distance	Interval

Total:

The Runner's Workout Log

Date		AM /PM

Warmup	Reps	Distance	Interval

Sets	Reps	Distance	Interval

Warmdown	Reps	Distance	Interval

Total:

The Runner's Workout Log

Date		AM /PM

Warmup	Reps	Distance	Interval

Sets	Reps	Distance	Interval

Warmdown	Reps	Distance	Interval

Total:

The Runner's Workout Log

Date		AM /PM

Warmup	**Reps**	**Distance**	**Interval**

Sets	**Reps**	**Distance**	**Interval**

Warmdown	**Reps**	**Distance**	**Interval**

Total:

The Runner's Workout Log

Date		AM /PM

Warmup	Reps	Distance	Interval

Sets	Reps	Distance	Interval

Warmdown	Reps	Distance	Interval

Total:

The Runner's Workout Log

Date		AM /PM

Warmup	Reps	Distance	Interval

Sets	Reps	Distance	Interval

Warmdown	Reps	Distance	Interval

Total:

The Runner's Workout Log

Date		AM /PM

Warmup	Reps	Distance	Interval

Sets	Reps	Distance	Interval

Warmdown	Reps	Distance	Interval

Total:

The Runner's Workout Log

Date		AM /PM

Warmup	Reps	Distance	Interval

Sets	Reps	Distance	Interval

Warmdown	Reps	Distance	Interval

Total:

The Runner's Workout Log

Date		AM /PM

Warmup	Reps	Distance	Interval

Sets	Reps	Distance	Interval

Warmdown	Reps	Distance	Interval

Total:

The Runner's Workout Log

Date		AM /PM

Warmup	Reps	Distance	Interval

Sets	Reps	Distance	Interval

Warmdown	Reps	Distance	Interval

Total:

The Runner's Workout Log

Date				AM /PM

Warmup	Reps	Distance	Interval

Sets	Reps	Distance	Interval

Warmdown	Reps	Distance	Interval

Total:

The Runner's Workout Log

Date		AM /PM

Warmup	Reps	Distance	Interval

Sets	Reps	Distance	Interval

Warmdown	Reps	Distance	Interval

Total:

The Runner's Workout Log

Date		AM /PM

Warmup	Reps	Distance	Interval

Sets	Reps	Distance	Interval

Warmdown	Reps	Distance	Interval

Total:

The Runner's Workout Log

Date		AM /PM

Warmup	Reps	Distance	Interval

Sets	Reps	Distance	Interval

Warmdown	Reps	Distance	Interval

Total:

The Runner's Workout Log

Date		AM /PM

Warmup	Reps	Distance	Interval

Sets	Reps	Distance	Interval

Warmdown	Reps	Distance	Interval

Total:

The Runner's Workout Log

Date		AM /PM

Warmup	Reps	Distance	Interval

Sets	Reps	Distance	Interval

Warmdown	Reps	Distance	Interval

Total:

The Runner's Workout Log

Date		AM /PM

Warmup	Reps	Distance	Interval

Sets	Reps	Distance	Interval

Warmdown	Reps	Distance	Interval

Total:

The Runner's Workout Log

Date		AM /PM

Warmup	Reps	Distance	Interval

Sets	Reps	Distance	Interval

Warmdown	Reps	Distance	Interval

Total:

The Runner's Workout Log

Date		AM /PM

Warmup	Reps	Distance	Interval

Sets	Reps	Distance	Interval

Warmdown	Reps	Distance	Interval

Total:

The Runner's Workout Log

Date		AM /PM

Warmup	Reps	Distance	Interval

Sets	Reps	Distance	Interval

Warmdown	Reps	Distance	Interval

Total:

PalladiumEducation.com

The Runner's Workout Log

Date		AM /PM

Warmup	Reps	Distance	Interval

Sets	Reps	Distance	Interval

Warmdown	Reps	Distance	Interval

Total:

The Runner's Workout Log

Date		AM /PM

Warmup	Reps	Distance	Interval

Sets	Reps	Distance	Interval

Warmdown	Reps	Distance	Interval

Total:

The Runner's Workout Log

Date		AM /PM

Warmup	Reps	Distance	Interval

Sets	Reps	Distance	Interval

Warmdown	Reps	Distance	Interval

Total:

Palladium Education,® Inc.

The Runner's Workout Log

Date		AM /PM

Warmup	Reps	Distance	Interval

Sets	Reps	Distance	Interval

Warmdown	Reps	Distance	Interval

Total:

The Runner's Workout Log

Date				AM /PM

Warmup	Reps	Distance	Interval

Sets	Reps	Distance	Interval

Warmdown	Reps	Distance	Interval

Total:

The Runner's Workout Log

Date		AM /PM

Warmup	Reps	Distance	Interval

Sets	Reps	Distance	Interval

Warmdown	Reps	Distance	Interval

Total:

The Runner's Workout Log

Date		AM /PM

Warmup	Reps	Distance	Interval

Sets	Reps	Distance	Interval

Warmdown	Reps	Distance	Interval

Total:

The Runner's Workout Log

Date				AM /PM
Warmup		**Reps**	**Distance**	**Interval**

Sets	**Reps**	**Distance**	**Interval**

Warmdown	**Reps**	**Distance**	**Interval**

Total:

The Runner's Workout Log

Date		AM /PM

Warmup	Reps	Distance	Interval

Sets	Reps	Distance	Interval

Warmdown	Reps	Distance	Interval

Total:

The Runner's Workout Log

Date		AM /PM

Warmup	Reps	Distance	Interval

Sets	Reps	Distance	Interval

Warmdown	Reps	Distance	Interval

Total:

The Runner's Workout Log

Date		AM /PM

Warmup	Reps	Distance	Interval

Sets	Reps	Distance	Interval

Warmdown	Reps	Distance	Interval

Total:

The Runner's Workout Log

Date		AM /PM

Warmup	**Reps**	**Distance**	**Interval**

Sets	**Reps**	**Distance**	**Interval**

Warmdown	**Reps**	**Distance**	**Interval**

Total:

PalladiumEducation.com

The Runner's Workout Log

Date		AM /PM

Warmup	Reps	Distance	Interval

Sets	Reps	Distance	Interval

Warmdown	Reps	Distance	Interval

Total:

The Runner's Workout Log

Date		AM /PM

Warmup	Reps	Distance	Interval

Sets	Reps	Distance	Interval

Warmdown	Reps	Distance	Interval

Total:

The Runner's Workout Log

Date		AM /PM

Warmup	Reps	Distance	Interval

Sets	Reps	Distance	Interval

Warmdown	Reps	Distance	Interval

Total:

The Runner's Workout Log

Date		AM /PM

Warmup	Reps	Distance	Interval

Sets	Reps	Distance	Interval

Warmdown	Reps	Distance	Interval

Total:

The Runner's Workout Log

Date		AM /PM

Warmup	Reps	Distance	Interval

Sets	Reps	Distance	Interval

Warmdown	Reps	Distance	Interval

Total:

The Runner's Workout Log

Date		AM /PM

Warmup	Reps	Distance	Interval

Sets	Reps	Distance	Interval

Warmdown	Reps	Distance	Interval

Total:

The Runner's Workout Log

Date		AM /PM

Warmup	Reps	Distance	Interval

Sets	Reps	Distance	Interval

Warmdown	Reps	Distance	Interval

Total:

The Runner's Workout Log

Date		AM /PM

Warmup	Reps	Distance	Interval

Sets	Reps	Distance	Interval

Warmdown	Reps	Distance	Interval

Total:

The Runner's Workout Log

Date		AM /PM

Warmup	Reps	Distance	Interval

Sets	Reps	Distance	Interval

Warmdown	Reps	Distance	Interval

Total:

The Runner's Workout Log

Date		AM /PM

Warmup	Reps	Distance	Interval

Sets	Reps	Distance	Interval

Warmdown	Reps	Distance	Interval

Total:

The Runner's Workout Log

Date		AM /PM

Warmup	Reps	Distance	Interval

Sets	Reps	Distance	Interval

Warmdown	Reps	Distance	Interval

Total:

The Runner's Workout Log

Date				AM /PM

Warmup	**Reps**	**Distance**	**Interval**

Sets	**Reps**	**Distance**	**Interval**

Warmdown	**Reps**	**Distance**	**Interval**

Total:

The Runner's Workout Log

Date		AM /PM

Warmup	Reps	Distance	Interval

Sets	Reps	Distance	Interval

Warmdown	Reps	Distance	Interval

Total:

Palladium Education,® Inc.

The Runner's Workout Log

Date		AM /PM

Warmup	Reps	Distance	Interval

Sets	Reps	Distance	Interval

Warmdown	Reps	Distance	Interval

Total:

The Runner's Workout Log

Date		AM /PM

Warmup	Reps	Distance	Interval

Sets	Reps	Distance	Interval

Warmdown	Reps	Distance	Interval

Total:

The Runner's Workout Log

Date		AM /PM

Warmup	Reps	Distance	Interval

Sets	Reps	Distance	Interval

Warmdown	Reps	Distance	Interval

Total:

The Runner's Workout Log

Date		AM /PM

Warmup	Reps	Distance	Interval

Sets	Reps	Distance	Interval

Warmdown	Reps	Distance	Interval

Total:

The Runner's Workout Log

Date		AM /PM

Warmup	Reps	Distance	Interval

Sets	Reps	Distance	Interval

Warmdown	Reps	Distance	Interval

Total:

The Runner's Workout Log

Date			AM /PM

Warmup	Reps	Distance	Interval

Sets	Reps	Distance	Interval

Warmdown	Reps	Distance	Interval

Total:

The Runner's Workout Log

Date		AM /PM

Warmup	Reps	Distance	Interval

Sets	Reps	Distance	Interval

Warmdown	Reps	Distance	Interval

Total:

PalladiumEducation.com

The Runner's Workout Log

Body Composition Log (skinfold) Measurements are in milimeters (mm)

Date	%	Triceps	Thigh	Suprailiac	Pectoral	Subscapula	Midaxilla	Abdomen

Body Measurements Log

Date	Neck	Chest	L. Arm	Abdomen	Hips	L. Thigh	L. Calf

PalladiumEducation.com

Weight Log

Date	Weight	Date	Weight

Weight Log

Date	Weight	Date	Weight

www.ingramcontent.com/pod-product-compliance
Lightning Source LLC
Chambersburg PA
CBHW071302040426
42444CB00009B/1842